A Page About Myself

Last year I read books about _____

_____

_____

This year I want to read books about _____

_____

_____

Last year I wrote stories about _____

_____

_____

This year I want to write stories about _____

_____

_____

Last year I enjoyed listening to stories about _____

_____

_____

This year I would like to listen to stories about _____

_____

_____

Summer Is Gone

Reread the poem "Now" and use your own ideas to complete the page.

Why do you think Prince Redcloud wrote this poem?

_____

_____

_____

What three things in your world make you think that summer
is about to arrive?

_____

_____

_____

What three things in your world make you think that summer is over?

_____

_____

_____

I would like to have summer all year long because _____

_____

_____

I would not like to have summer all year long because _____

_____

The Fall Fair

Use information from the poem "September" and your own ideas to complete the page.

Things I would want to see at the fair:

_____

_____

_____

_____

_____

Things I would not want to see at the fair:

_____

_____

_____

_____

_____

Three things I would be surprised to see at the fair:

_____

_____

_____

BINGO

11	13	24	31	46
6	9	27	37	50
9	19	21	34	48
3	21	22	32	45
4	12	23	35	39

Rhubarb Jam

Sweet Pickles

Hot Dog Words

Use the clues to complete the words.

CLUES

1. the opposite of water

2. the opposite of soft

3. an animal that says "Quack"

4. an animal with a long tail

5. the opposite of first

6. a place to make wishes

7. a kind of plane

8. what you do to an apple
   in a tree

9. not very much—a little

10. a big stone

11. like a wigwam

12. the opposite of stand

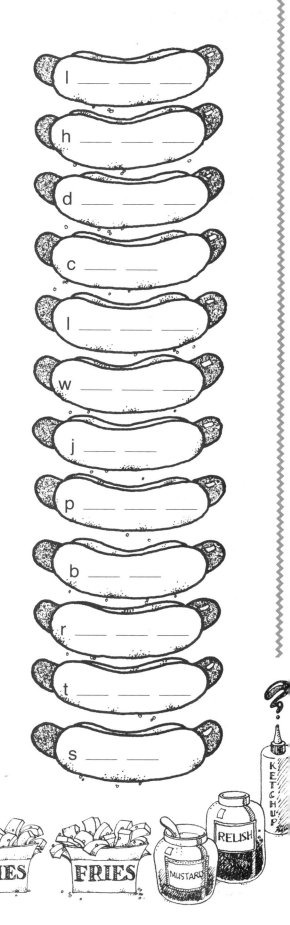

Hit the Target

Print letters to make rhyming words in each target.

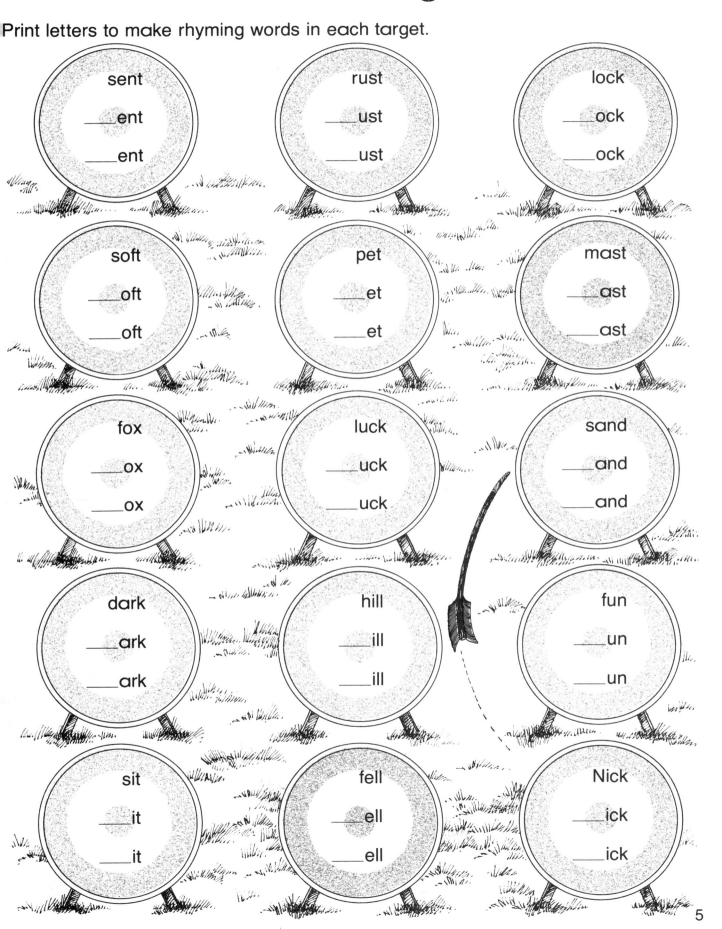

sent
___ent
___ent

rust
___ust
___ust

lock
___ock
___ock

soft
___oft
___oft

pet
___et
___et

mast
___ast
___ast

fox
___ox
___ox

luck
___uck
___uck

sand
___and
___and

dark
___ark
___ark

hill
___ill
___ill

fun
___un
___un

sit
___it
___it

fell
___ell
___ell

Nick
___ick
___ick

5

Zoo Sounds

Complete the sentences.
Try to think of a different answer each time.

Example:

I couldn't hear the apes _gibber_

because _they were eating bananas._

I could hear the bees _____

because _____

I couldn't hear the cattle _____

because _____

I could hear the doves _____

because _____

I couldn't hear the elephants _____

because _____

I could hear the frogs _____

because _____

I couldn't hear the geese _____

because _____

I could hear the hyenas _____

because _____

6

couldn't hear the iguanas _____

because _____

could hear the jackals _____

because _____

couldn't hear the kiwi birds _____

because _____

could hear the lions _____

because _____

couldn't hear the monkeys _____

because _____

could hear the nightingales _____

cause _____

ouldn't hear the owls _____

cause _____

ould hear the puppies _____

cause _____

ouldn't hear the quails _____

cause _____

I could hear the rabbits _____

because _____

I couldn't hear the snakes _____

because _____

I could hear the tigers _____

because _____

I couldn't hear the umbrella birds _____

because _____

I could hear the vultures _____

because _____

I couldn't hear the wolves _____

because _____

I could hear the x-ray fish _____

because _____

I couldn't hear the yaks _____

because _____

I could hear the zebras _____

because _____

Puzzle Fun

Print the answers to these riddles.

the sound bees make   — — — — —

a toy for a baby   — — — — — —

the opposite of high   — — —

another word for yell   — — — — —

a musical instrument   — — — — — — —

baby dogs   — — — — — — —

the opposite of cry   — — — —

a wise bird   — — —

the king of beasts   — — — —

a grown-up bunny   — — — — — —

Find and circle your answers in the word search.

s	e	l	a	u	g	h	r
p	c	l	o	w	g	x	a
b	e	r	a	b	b	i	t
u	o	x	e	e	b	s	t
z	w	s	a	a	i	l	l
z	l	i	o	n	m	r	e
p	u	p	p	i	e	s	q
t	r	u	m	p	e	t	x

9

By Myself

Use information from the story "Home Alone" and your own ideas to complete the page.

Why is today different for Andy?

_____

_____

_____

Why does Andy have two keys to get into his home?

_____

_____

_____

What does Andy do on different days after school?

_____

_____

_____

How does Andy help his mother when he gets home?

_____

_____

What are some things that Andy could do to amuse himself
until his mother gets home?

_____

_____

_____

What things could Andy and his mother do on a day
when she does not have to work?

_____

_____

_____

Write a message that Andy could have written his mother
from a person who phoned.

_____

_____

_____

Write a note that Andy might write for his mother to read
when she gets home from work.

_____

_____

_____

On His Own

Complete each sentence by printing your answer on the line.

(left heft)

Andy _____ school to go home.

(grab drab lab)

He made a _____ for his coat.

(Bill still will)

Andy did not stand _____

(stop drop pop)

He kept going and did not _____ walking.

(pond blond bond)

Andy went past the _____ very quickly.

(dwell smell well)   (skunk bunk hunk)

There was the _____ of a _____

(frill till hill)   (met pet fret)

He went up the _____ and at home he _____ Bisquits.

(ten Ben men)

He was glad to find his _____ toy animals waiting for him.

(trip drip lip)

He didn't have to go on a _____ to the zoo to see animals.

(at fat chat)

He had his own animals _____ home.

Andy's Note

Andy wrote a note to his mother. He made some spelling mistakes.
Print the words correctly on the lines below the note.

Dear Mom,

I came home on time **todae** and got **yor** note on the **tabel**.
My **freind** Tony invited me over to his **plase** to practise **socer**.
Bisquits was **hungary**, so I fed her.

A lady called you but she **did'nt** want to **leaf** a message.
The **hambergers** are defrosting on the **countor**.
I promise **two** clean my room and be on time for **super**.
I want to tell you about my **excting** day at **scool**
and show you the town that I **bilt.**

Lve,
Andy

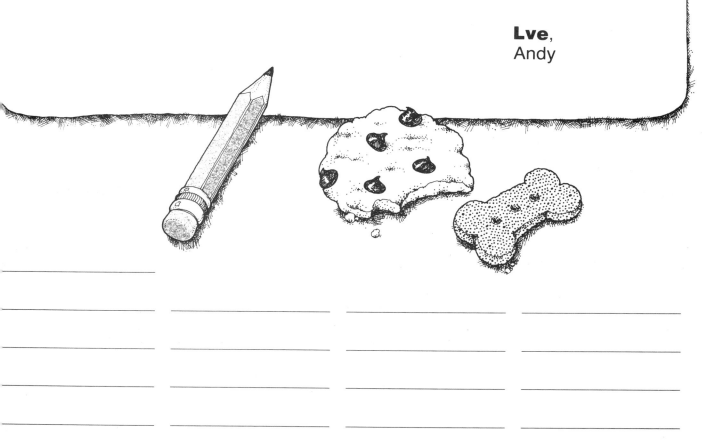

_____

_____   _____   _____

_____   _____   _____

_____   _____   _____

Bathtub Play

Use information from the poem "One Snail and Me" to answer the questions.

What did the snail do?

_____

_____

Why wouldn't the turtles leave their shells?

_____

_____

Where did the ducks swim?

_____

_____

What did the seals do in the tub?

_____

_____

_____

_____

Why did the whales spout and pout?

_____

_____

Where were the kangaroos dressed to go?

_____

_____

What did the bears love to eat?

_____

_____

Why don't people like big alligators?

_____

_____

What happened when nine hippopotamuses tried to get in the tub?

_____

_____

What did the little minnows do?

_____

_____

Bubble Bath Time

Choose letters from the list to make words.

ch   sh   th   wh

___ ___ort   fi___ ___   bea___ ___   ___ ___ale   ___ ___ink

___ ___eel   wit___ ___   lun___ ___   ___ ___ell   bru___ ___

___ ___ird   ba___ ___   di___ ___   ___ ___ank   mo___ ___er

Choose some of the above words to complete the sentences.

1. We found a beautiful _____ on the sandy _____

2. My father and _____ are going on a trip.

3. I used a _____ on my hair.

4. I had soup and a _____ of ice cream for _____

5. The _____ on my bike is broken.

6. I am in the _____ grade at school.

7. I _____ he is too _____ to reach the door.

8. The _____ spouted and pouted.

9. I filled the tub with water for my _____

10. We are going to the lake to catch _____

16

Left Behind

Everyone came back to get the things that were left behind in the bathtub.

Example:

The shell belonged to the turtle.

It was the ___turtle's___ shell.

The lunch belonged to the seal.

It was the _____

The umbrella belonged to the kangaroo.

It was the _____

The honeyjar belonged to the bear.

It was the _____

What things could be found in your bathroom that belong to someone else?

Example:

1. ___Dad's___ ___towel___

2. _____ _____

3. _____ _____

4. _____ _____

5. _____ _____

6. _____ _____

What to Name a Fish

Reread the poem, and answer the following questions.

What names does the poet think a fish might be given?

_____   _____

_____   _____

Why does the poet think that a fish doesn't care what its name is?

_____

_____

Describe these strange fish:

The Orange Weed-Killer

_____

_____

The Tiny Spotted Garbage Fish

_____

_____

Write a poem about a fish with a special name.

"My name is _____," said the little fish.
"There are two things I want, if I could have a wish:

_____

_____

(Of course if fishes had wishes, what a strange world it would be.)

Catching Minnows

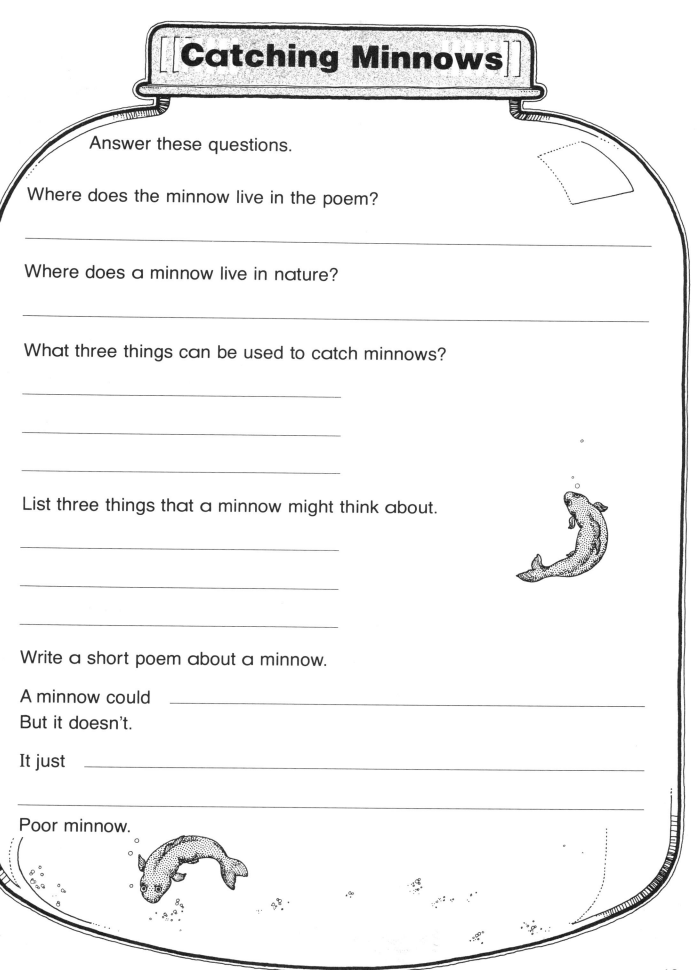

Answer these questions.

Where does the minnow live in the poem?

_____

Where does a minnow live in nature?

_____

What three things can be used to catch minnows?

_____

_____

_____

List three things that a minnow might think about.

_____

_____

_____

Write a short poem about a minnow.

A minnow could _____

But it doesn't.

It just _____

_____

Poor minnow.

A Salmon for Simon

Use information from the story to answer these questions.

When Simon was little, how did he catch minnows?

_____

Why were many salmon swimming past the island?

_____

_____

How did the gulls get the clams out of their shells?

_____

_____

Who caught the salmon?

_____

Why did Simon want to save the salmon?

_____

_____

How did Simon save the salmon?

_____

_____

_____

Do you think Simon will catch other fish?

_____

_____

_____

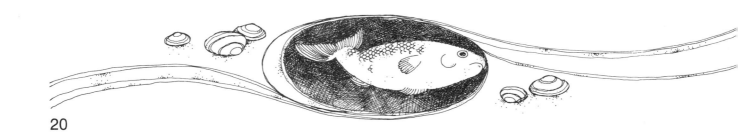

Fishing for Words

Use the words in the list to complete Simon's story.

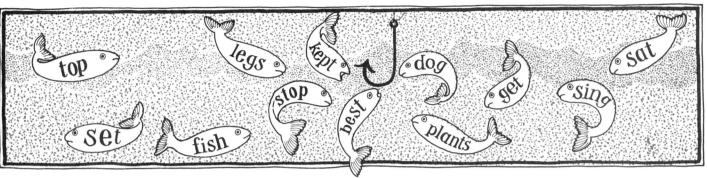

One day Simon went fishing.
Simon did not stand up with his fishing pole.

Instead, he _____ down on the shore

beside the green trees and the _____

He _____ the fishing pole between two rocks.

Simon crossed his _____ and waited.

He started to _____ a song to himself.

He _____ watching the _____ of the water
to see if his line was bobbing up and down.

Simon knew that the biggest and the _____ fish

often _____ away.

He hoped that one _____ would _____
to eat the worm on his hook.
Soon Simon caught a fish. It was a salmon!

Simon planned to keep the salmon for his _____
Simon felt like a great fisherman.

Catch a Word

Find the words in the list that make the underlined sound in each word.
Print these words in the list they belong to.

bed	mop	gum	cat	fish
_____	_____	_____	_____	_____
_____	_____	_____	_____	_____
_____	_____	_____	_____	_____
_____	_____	_____	_____	_____
_____	_____	_____	_____	_____

get	leg	cut	stop	kept	bill	dog	win	top
sing	fun	bat	plants	sat	set	best	spin
sad	frog	shut	off	lung	grab	hum	in

Add your own words.

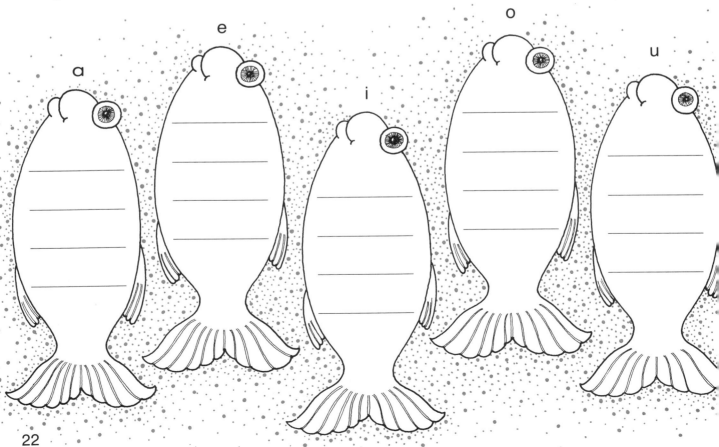

a

e

i

o

u

Fill a Salmon

Use the list of letters to complete the words.

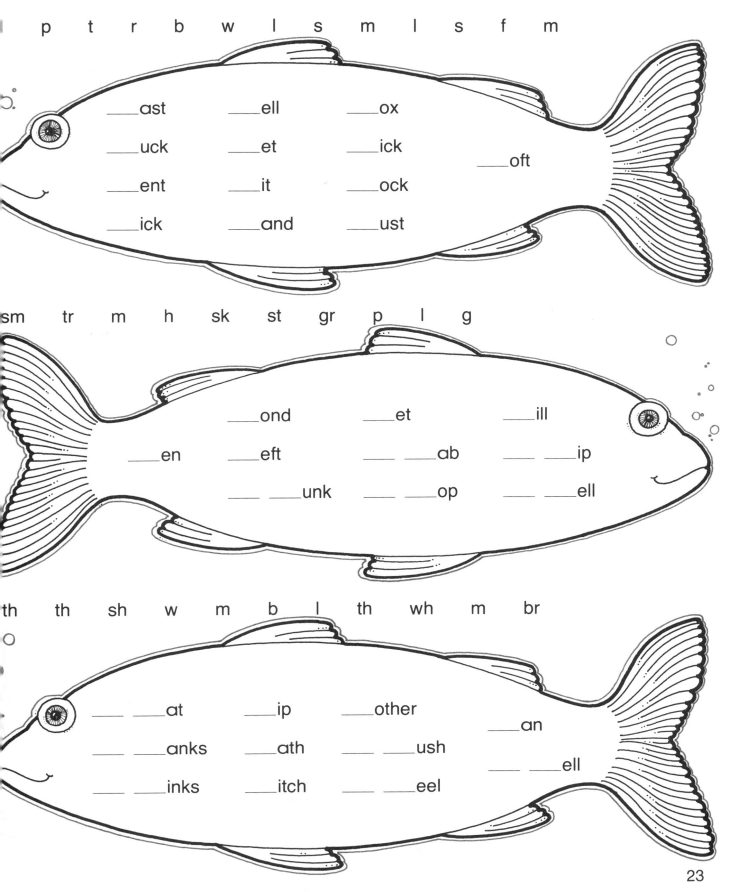

p   t   r   b   w   l   s   m   l   s   f   m

___ast   ___ell   ___ox

___uck   ___et   ___ick

                                      ___oft

___ent   ___it   ___ock

___ick   ___and   ___ust

sm   tr   m   h   sk   st   gr   p   l   g

___ond   ___et   ___ill

___en   ___eft   ___ ___ab   ___ ___ip

___ ___unk   ___ ___op   ___ ___ell

th   th   sh   w   m   b   l   th   wh   m   br

___ ___at   ___ip   ___other

                                      ___an

___ ___anks   ___ath   ___ ___ush

                                      ___ ___ell

___ ___inks   ___itch   ___ ___eel

Sludge's Story

The story "Nate the Great Goes Undercover" was told by Nate, the boy detective. How would Sludge have told Nate's story? Rewrite the story in Sludge's words.

_____

_____

_____

_____

_____

_____

_____

_____

_____

_____

_____

_____

_____

_____

Word Clues

Can you solve these cases?

Case 1: Nate says, "Join the letters that go together to make a word."

g	ire	s	oke
d	ive	s	ure
t	ame	br	ame

Case 2: Nate says, "Add the missing letter to make a word."

sc___red   cl___thes

k___te   tr___e

sn___ke   t___me

m___re   ___se

N___te   c___se

Case 3: Nate says, "Add the missing letters to make a word."

m___l___   c___v___

f___r___   wh___l___

pl___t___   th___s___

c___s___   s___r___

Nate's Riddles

Can you answer these riddles that Nate wrote?
Try not to look at the answers unless you have to.

What is the name of something used to sit on?

_____

What is the name of a sandy place by a lake?

_____

What is another word for "yes"?

_____

What is a word that rhymes with "hay"?

_____

What has 365 days in it?

_____

What do mice like to eat?

_____

What do you brush three times a day?

_____

What is the opposite of "make-believe"?

_____

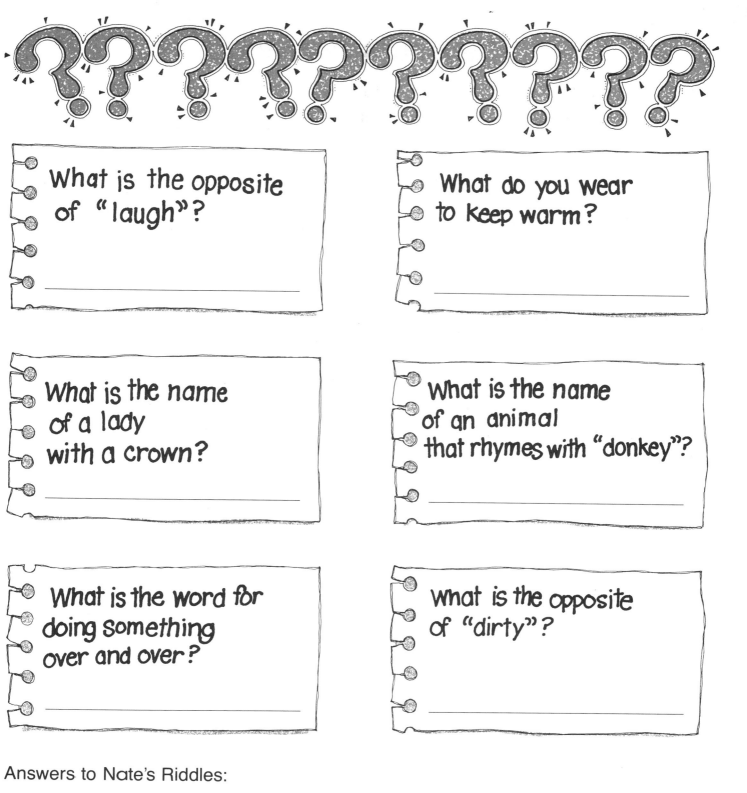

What is the opposite of "laugh"?

_____

What do you wear to keep warm?

_____

What is the name of a lady with a crown?

_____

What is the name of an animal that rhymes with "donkey"?

_____

What is the word for doing something over and over?

_____

What is the opposite of "dirty"?

_____

Answers to Nate's Riddles:

| clean | monkey | stay | real | coat | chair | queen |
| year | cheese | again | teeth | beach | okay | cry |

My Skipping Song

Use your own ideas to complete the poem.

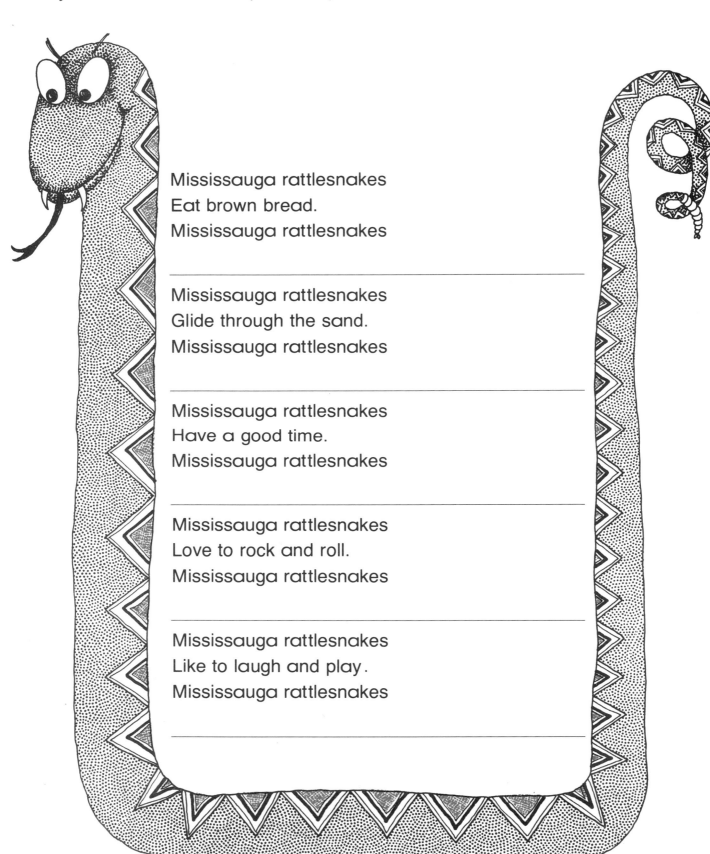

Mississauga rattlesnakes
Eat brown bread.
Mississauga rattlesnakes

_____

Mississauga rattlesnakes
Glide through the sand.
Mississauga rattlesnakes

_____

Mississauga rattlesnakes
Have a good time.
Mississauga rattlesnakes

_____

Mississauga rattlesnakes
Love to rock and roll.
Mississauga rattlesnakes

_____

Mississauga rattlesnakes
Like to laugh and play.
Mississauga rattlesnakes

_____

Rhyming Words

Print two words that rhyme with each of the words below.

bread   _____   _____

eat   _____   _____

rattle   _____   _____

snake   _____   _____

glide   _____   _____

ime   _____   _____

play   _____   _____

honey   _____   _____

brown   _____   _____

Can you think of some words that almost rhyme with rattlesnake?

Example:

piece of cake
_____

_____

_____

Can you think of a word
that almost rhymes with Mississauga?

_____

Molly and the Giant

These sentences are from the story "Molly Whuppie Fights the Giant."
Write a number beside each sentence in the order that the story happened.

☐ She married the King's youngest son.

☐ He took the three youngest children, and left them alone in the forest.

☐ First she tugged softly at the ring.

☐ In the middle of the night, the giant tiptoed into the room.

☐ Then Mollie carried off the sword to the King.

☐ The wife put the whole six of them into the same bed.

☐ Her second sister married his second son.

☐ Molly said, "I would bundle you up into a sack."

☐ She felt the purse under the pillow.

☐ At day break, they came to another house.

☐ There was an old woodcutter who had many children.

☐ The children ate the bread and treacle.

☐ And soon, her eldest sister married the King's eldest son.

☐ But Molly laughed and said: "Maybe twice I'll come to see you, and maybe once again."

☐ He gripped her and lifted her clean up into the dark over his head.

Molly's Rhyme Time

Print a rhyming word on each line to complete the sentences.

It's _____ if you _____

                                                                  okay
  stay
  tray

Have you _____ to see the _____

  been
  clean
  queen

She _____ to help the boy who _____

  cried
  tried
  fried

I'll _____ you to swim at the _____

  reach
  teach
  beach

Mother cut my _____ in the _____

  fair
  hair
  chair

The _____ was eating my _____

  coat
  throat
  goat

Did it _____ _____

  pain
  rain
  again

Story Numbers

Use information from the story "Molly Whuppie Fights the Giant" and your own ideas to complete the page.

In the story there was one hero by the name of _____

There were six children because _____

_____

There were two kinds of necklaces because _____

_____

The giant owned three things because _____

_____

The King had three sons because _____

_____

_____

Molly said to the giant, "Four times is enough for all" because _____

_____

_____

A story that has the number seven in it is _____

_____

My lucky number is ____ because _____

_____

Molly's Word Sacks

Find the words in the list that make the same sound
and have the same letters as the underlined letters.
Print these words in the sack they belong to.
Add words to each list.

why   thief   any   lady   field   ago
also   cookie   every   pie   sky   cried

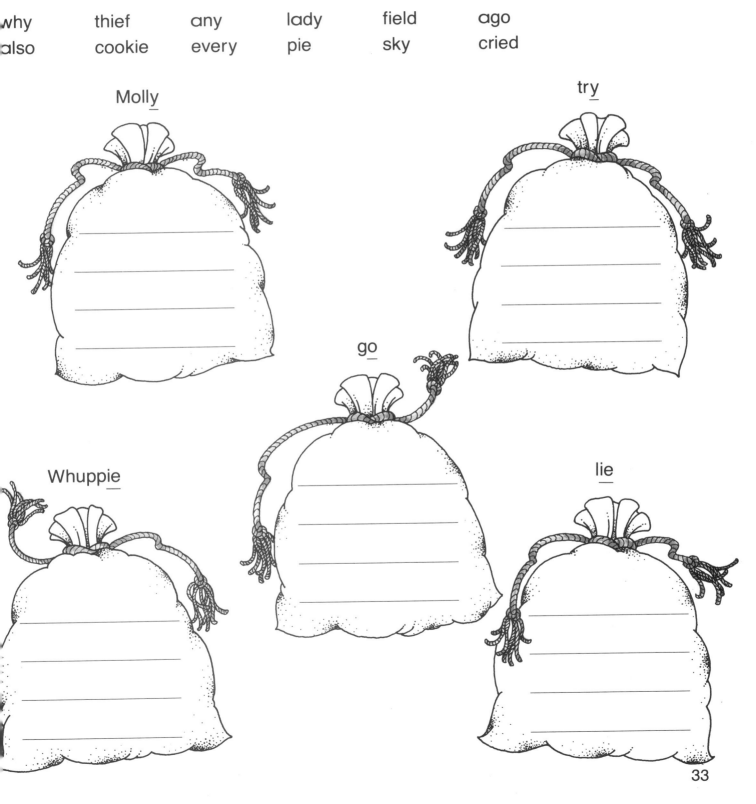

Molly

try

go

Whuppie

lie

Trading for a Living

Use information from the story "The Ox-Cart Man" to complete the page.

Five things that the ox-cart man packed to take to market were:

_____

_____

_____

_____

Three things that the ox-cart man sold that he didn't pack were:

_____

_____

_____

The ox-cart man bought gifts for everyone in his family.

He bought _____

_____

_____

_____

I am like the ox-cart man because _____

_____

Trading Things

Write a trading poem about things that could have been traded in the olden days.

An old man traded a cow

for a _____

Then he traded that _____

for a _____

Then he traded that _____

for a _____

Then he traded that _____

for a _____

Then he traded that _____

for a _____

Then he traded that _____

for a _____

Then he traded that _____

for a _____

Then he traded that _____

for a _____

Finally, he traded that _____ for a cow.
Wow!

Trading Words

Make rhyming words.

rake

_____

_____

_____

_____

_____

game

_____

_____

_____

_____

_____

pole

_____

_____

_____

_____

_____

fire

_____

_____

_____

_____

_____

wade

_____

_____

_____

_____

_____

joke

_____

_____

_____

_____

_____

A Full Cart

This is a list of everything that the ox-cart man sold.
Arrange the list in alphabetical order.

feathers

potatoes

wool

mittens

brooms

box

bag

shawl

candles

shingles

apples

honey

honeycombs

harness

barrel

ox

ox cart

yoke

maple sugar

cabbages

turnips

Listen for the Sound

Find the words in the list that make the sound that is underlined in each word.
Print the words in the correct column.

lake	kite	bone	glue
_____	_____	_____	_____
_____	_____	_____	_____
_____	_____	_____	_____
_____	_____	_____	_____

hole   use   nose   nine   grade   name   bite   cave   side   clothes
sure   while   game   true   broke   blue   time   scare   woke   Sue

chair	day	queen	beach
_____	_____	_____	_____
_____	_____	_____	_____
_____	_____	_____	_____
_____	_____	_____	_____

clean   teeth   stay   pair   beads   feet   way   flair   okay   cheese
fair   read   pay   been   wheat   air   play   seen   hair   plead

Use information from the story "There's a Party at Mona's Tonight" and your own ideas to complete the page.

Why didn't Mona invite Potter Pig to the party?

_____

_____

What happened the first time Potter knocked at Mona's door?

_____

_____

What did Potter mean when he said, "I'm always the life of the party"?

_____

_____

What mistake did Potter make after Mona asked him to the party?

_____

_____

If Potter had used my plan, he might have gotten into the party:

_____

_____

_____

_____

Potter Pig's Puzzle

Can you find and circle 16 words in the word search?

s	t	r	e	e	t	x	f	e	d	t
t	p	s	h	r	u	b	y	w	x	g
r	s	l	t	r	s	p	o	o	l	o
e	x	m	i	p	p	c	o	o	k	o
a	f	k	t	t	r	r	s	o	v	s
m	b	o	o	k	i	w	o	o	d	e
s	c	r	e	w	h	r	o	o	m	w
t	h	r	o	u	g	h	k	l	x	x
w	o	o	l	x	b	r	o	o	m	s

Make a word search for a friend.
Use words from the story "There's a Party at Mona's Tonight."

xpbcrw ?

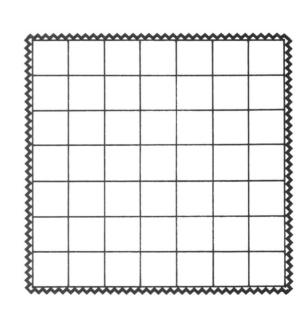

40

Words

In the story "There's a Party at Mona's Tonight," there are some interesting words.
Look up the following words in the story to discover how each one is used
in a sentence. Write the meaning for each word.

guppies: _____

invitation: _____

_____

cocoa: _____

by hook or by crook: _____

_____

statue: _____

sneezed: _____

bagpiper: _____

tunnel: _____

gas meter: _____

dirigible: _____

bamboozle: _____

fandango: _____

 # The Thin Man

Use information from the poem "I'm Skeleton" and your own ideas
to complete the page.

I live around here because _____

_____

I scare _____

When people see me, they _____ and _____

and _____

Oops, there's a dog, _____

because _____

_____

What do you think?

Two songs a skeleton would like to hear are:

_____

_____

Two movies a skeleton would like to see are:

_____

_____

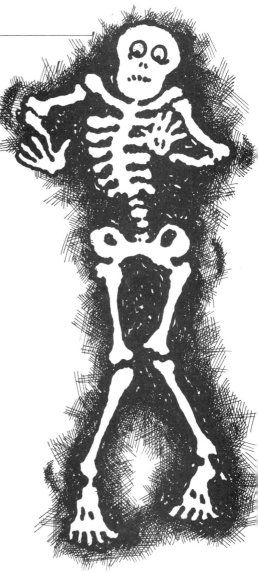

Shopping Problems

Use information from the poem "Witch Goes Shopping" and your own ideas to complete the page.

Here is the witch's shopping list:

_____

_____

_____

_____

_____

_____

_____

The witch complained about the store to the owner. She said, _____

_____

_____

The witch could not get what she wanted to cook with at the store.

Instead she used _____

_____

Three places the witch should have gone shopping are:

_____

_____

_____

Who's There?

In the poem "No One," you do not know who blew out the candle. Pretend that you know and write a story about what happened.

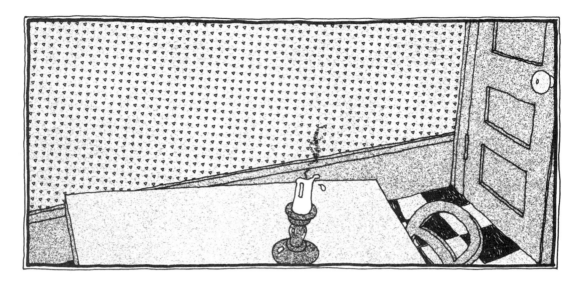

In that room, only I know who blew out the candle.

_____

_____

_____

_____

_____

_____

_____

_____

_____

_____

_____

The Country or the City?

Use information from the poem "Dear Country Witch" and your own ideas to complete the page.

City Witch thinks that a city Halloween is better because _____

_____

City Witch says that in the city they will be able to _____

_____

_____

Write a letter from Country Witch to City Witch.

Dear City Witch,

_____

_____

_____

_____

In the country we will be able to _____

_____

_____

_____

Your friend,
Country Witch

Sleepy-Time Stories

Use your own ideas to complete the page.

Make a list of stories that the witch's child likes to hear at bedtime.

_____

_____

_____

_____

_____

Make a list of shows that the witch's child likes to watch on television.

_____

_____

_____

_____

Make a list of games that the witch's child likes to play.

_____

_____

_____

_____

Scary Words

You can have fun printing words the way they are printed in the poem "Old Devil Wind." Use the words in the list.

strap   street   wool   broom   screw   wood

scratch   hood   loose   pool   goose   foot

book   spring   room   hook   spray

Print all the words that make the 'oo' sound, as in "foot."
Print these words the way the word "swish" is printed.

_____   _____   _____

_____   _____   _____

Print all the words that make the 'oo' sound as in "pool."
Print these words the way the word "creak" is printed.

_____   _____   _____

_____   _____   _____

Print all the words that start with these letters: "str", "scr", "spr".
Print these words the way the word "thump" is printed.

_____   _____   _____

_____   _____   _____

A Windy Day

What does each thing do in the poem "Old Devil Wind"?

Ghost began to _____

Stool began to _____

Broom began to _____

Candle began to _____

Fire began to _____

Window began to _____

Floor began to _____

Door began to _____

Owl began to _____

Witch began to _____

_____

Wind began to _____

And Wind blew away _____

_____

_____

_____

_____

The Big Wind

Complete this story about the biggest wind in the world.

The wind began to moan.
Then, it began to wail.
Then, it began to scream.

All of a sudden, it began to blow the trees so hard that they _____

_____

_____

Then it spotted the roofs of the houses and began to _____

_____

_____

Next, it saw some children on the way home and it began to _____

_____

_____

It found some cows in a field, _____

_____

It saw a little town beside a mountain _____

_____

Then it decided to blow away the mountain but instead _____

_____

And that was the end of the wind!

Haunted Houses

Print the words in alphabetical order in each haunted house.

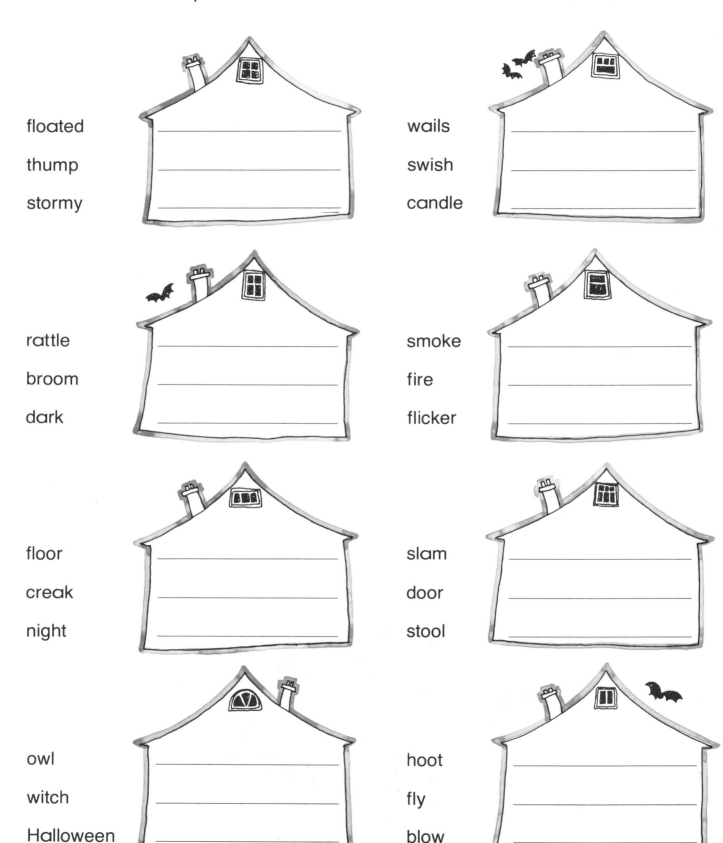

floated

thump

stormy

wails

swish

candle

rattle

broom

dark

smoke

fire

flicker

floor

creak

night

slam

door

stool

owl

witch

Halloween

hoot

fly

blow

Joining Up

Join two words with a line to make one word.

base	one	an	one
some	self	every	self
him	ball	my	other

after	noon	in	side
in	thing	any	thing
every	side	out	to

Make one word by putting two words together.

_____   _____

_____   _____

_____   _____

_____   _____

Use one of the words you made in a sentence.

_____

_____

Too Much to Eat

Use information from the story "Yummers" to answer the questions.

Why was Emily upset?

_____

_____

What was the first exercise that Emily tried?

_____

_____

Why was walking not a good exercise for Emily?

_____

_____

What kind of sandwiches did Emily choose?

_____

_____

What was special about corn-on-the-cob?

_____

_____

What did Emily have on her hot scones?

_____

Who didn't like eskimo pies?

_____

Why did Eugene buy Girl Scout cookies?

_____

_____

What did Emily eat at the drugstore?

_____

_____

What free product did Emily sample at the supermarket?

_____

What two things did Emily eat in the park?

_____

_____

What advice did Eugene give Emily?

_____

_____

In the Park

Circle a word to complete each sentence.

One day Emily got (dresses, dressed, dressing) to go outside.

She (walks, walked, walking) down the street.

Emily (listens, listened, listening) to the birds along the way.

Emily (stops, stopped, stopping) at Eugene's house.

She (invites, invited, inviting) Eugene to join her in the park.

Eugene (fills, filled, filling) a basket with food for a picnic.

He (carries, carried, carrying) the basket to the park.

At the park they (plays, played, playing) ball.

They (dive, dived, diving) into the water to swim.

Later they (opens, opened, opening) the basket and had a picnic.

Eugene and Emily (finishes, finished, finishing) their picnic.

They (crosses, crossed, crossing) the river in the park
on their way home.

The two friends (enjoys, enjoyed, enjoying) their day.

A Secret in My Sandwich

Secret codes are fun to write! To use the code you match a number with a letter to make a word. Here is the secret code.

1	2	3	4	5	6	7	8	9	10	11	12	13
A	B	C	D	E	F	G	H	I	J	K	L	M
14	15	16	17	18	19	20	21	22	23	24	25	26
N	O	P	Q	R	S	T	U	V	W	X	Y	Z

Use the secret code to find out what this message says.

9   1 13   16 18 15 21 4   15 6   20 8 5   19 1 14 4 23 9 3 8

___   ___   _____   _____   _____   _____

13 25   6 1 20 8 5 18   13 1 4 5   6 15 18   13 5

_____   _____   _____   _____   ____

22 9 14 3 5 14 26 15

_____

Use the secret code to print these words in code.

turns	jumped	doing
_____	_____	_____
loves	finished	eating
_____	_____	_____
walks	wished	crying
_____	_____	_____

Lunch Time

Use information from the story "The Sandwich" and your own ideas
to complete the page.

Write five things that you have learned about Vincenzo
from the first two pages of the story.

_____

_____

_____

_____

_____

Write five things that you would put in the first two pages of a story
about your life.

_____

_____

_____

_____

_____

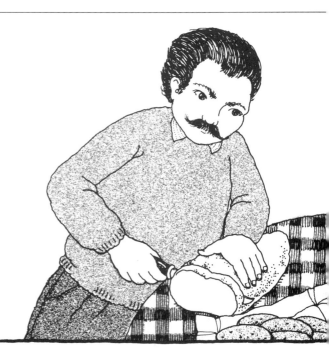

Write five things that Vincenzo and his father did when they made their lunches.

_____

_____

_____

_____

_____

Write five things about making or eating your own lunch.

_____

_____

_____

_____

_____

Invent the biggest sandwich in the world. What would it be made of?

_____

_____

_____

_____

The Lunch Room

You are going to write a play. Use the words that are spoken on pages 120–122 in the story "The Sandwich."

Example:

Matt: _Vincenzo! Come'n eat with us!_

Vincenzo: _____

Rita: _____

Vincenzo: _____

_____

_____

Rita: _____

_____

Vincenzo: _____

Paul: _____

Rita: _____

_____

_____

Cindy: _____

Matt: _____

_____

Rita: _____

Matt: _____

Matt: _____

Rita, Hans, Paul, and Cindy: _____

Questions, Questions

why   what   where   when   how   who   which

Using the words above, write two questions you would ask each of the following.

A cook

1. _____

2. _____

A snowman

1. _____

2. _____

A robin

1. _____

2. _____

A crocodile

1. _____

2. _____

Chicken Soup with Rice

Write a calendar poem using your own words.

In January it's so nice

_____

_____

In February it will be

_____

_____

In March the wind blows

_____

_____

In April I will go away

_____

_____

In May I truly think it best

_____

_____

In June I saw a charming group

_____

_____

In July I'll take a peep

_____

_____

In August it will be so hot

_____

_____

In September I will ride

_____

_____

In October I'll be a host

_____

_____

In November's gusty gale

_____

_____

In December I will be

_____

_____

Adding Letters

Make words by putting two groups of letters together.

Example:

for + est = _____forest_____

a + go = _____   hun + dred = _____

dra + gon = _____   in + side = _____

vi + sit = _____   un + til = _____

a + long = _____   kit + tens = _____

an + gry = _____   a + sleep = _____

be + fore = _____   can + dy = _____

sud + den + ly = _____

Can you think of some groups of letters that go together to make words?

_____ + _____ = _____

_____ + _____ = _____

A Surprise for Lunch

Use your own ideas to complete the page.

What is your anything sandwich?

_____

_____

My friend's favourite sandwich is _____

_____

_____

If I mailed anyone a sandwich it would be _____

_____

_____

because _____

_____

Here is how the sandwich was invented:

_____

_____

_____

A Lunch Bag Full of Words

Find and circle 20 words in the word search.

c	o	o	k	i	e	n	h
s	a	n	d	w	i	c	h
u	p	b	r	e	a	d	m
g	p	o	t	a	t	o	r
a	l	u	n	c	h	l	t
r	e	p	j	a	m	b	n
l	p	i	e	k	w	a	r
i	p	k	t	e	g	g	s
c	b	a	n	a	n	a	x
l	e	m	o	n	i	o	n
o	r	a	n	g	e	x	x
m	i	l	k	p	e	a	r
g	r	a	p	e	s	s	s

Ma Minnie's Story

Complete these sentences in order to tell Ma Minnie's story.

Hello! My name is _____

I live in a little _____

I make _____ and _____ for my living.

_____ and _____ all day long.

I buy _____ to make coconut cakes.

I fell and spilled the _____

A monkey saw me licking my _____

The monkey thought that I called the molasses _____

He asked for some _____ at the store.

The customers all _____

The shopkeeper gave him a _____

The monkey opened the bag and out _____

_____

The monkey picked a fruit. It was a _____

And that is how trouble made the _____

Ma Minnie's Secret Code

Use this code to print the secret words below. To use the code, match a number with a group of letters to make a word.

1	2	3	4	5	6	7	8	9	10	11	12	13
mon	sell	vil	sit	cus	re	mov	des	ers	ber	a	ed	be

14	15	16	17	18	19	20	21	22	23	24	25	26
mem	tom	rush	key	stop	ting	turn	ing	tion	lage	neath	pep	per

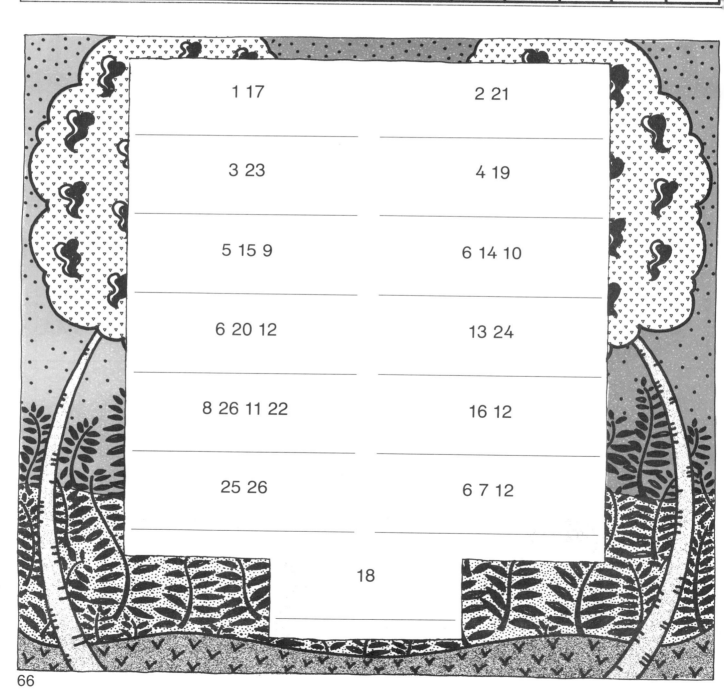

1 17 _____   2 21 _____

3 23 _____   4 19 _____

5 15 9 _____   6 14 10 _____

6 20 12 _____   13 24 _____

8 26 11 22 _____   16 12 _____

25 26 _____   6 7 12 _____

18 _____

Do You Know What Happened?

Write ten things in the order that they happened in the story "How Trouble Made the Monkey Eat Pepper."

1. Ma Minnie sold delicious cakes.

2. _____

3. _____

4. _____
   _____

5. _____
   _____

6. _____
   _____

7. _____
   _____

8. _____
   _____

9. _____
   _____

10. _____
    _____

Monkey Changes

Change the underlined letters in these words to make new words.

throat   splash   sprung   scrap

_____   _____   _____   _____

shrink   string   three   stroll

_____   _____   _____   _____

═══

myself   anything   everybody   football

_____   _____   _____   _____

birthday   homework   headline   sunshine

_____   _____   _____   _____

═══

camps   loves   eats   jumps

_____   _____   _____   _____

lived   rushed   stayed   stopped

_____   _____   _____   _____

hunting   talking   walking   wishing

_____   _____   _____   _____

Food Fun

Some foods that we like make funny sounds when we eat them.
Write a poem using the sounds that food makes when you eat it.

I like to munch potato chips because they crunch.

I like to munch _____ because they _____

I like to munch _____ because they _____

I like to munch _____ because they _____

I like to munch _____ because they _____

I like to munch _____ because they _____

I like to munch _____ because they _____

I like to munch _____ because they _____

What do you think?

The noisiest food I eat is _____

The quietest food I eat is _____

The tiniest food I eat is _____

The biggest food I eat is _____

Food War

Use the poem "Apple War" as a pattern for your own poem.
Write a new poem by writing different words on the lines.

One, two, three, four,

They _____ past my door,

One, two, three, four,

They _____ into the grocery store,

One, two, three, four,

They _____, not a cent more.

One, two, three, four,

They _____ rotten to the core,

One, two, three, four,

They _____ of the grocery store,

One, two, three, four,

They _____ past my door,

One, two, three, four,

They _____ war.

Thinking about Food

Use your own ideas to complete the page.

What food comes in a yellow package made by nature?

_____

What food comes in bunches?

_____

What food breaks?

_____

What food spills?

_____

What food is frozen?

_____

What food makes you laugh?

_____

What food makes you cry?

_____

What food grows on trees?

_____

What food grows underground?

_____

I Am Always Hungry

In the poem "My Mouth," the poet says that he loves to eat all the time.
When are you hungry? Write your own poem about food.

i love to eat _____
when i am alone

i love to eat _____
when i am sad

i love to eat _____
when i am glad

i love to eat _____
when i am full (i think)

i love to eat _____

when i am _____

i love to eat _____

when i am _____

i love to eat _____

when i am _____

i love to eat _____

when i am _____

Crumbs

Use information from the poem "Revenge" and your own ideas to complete the page.

Who do you think took the last cookie out of the cookie jar?

_____

What kind of cookies could they have been?

_____

Where is the person in the poem going to put the cookie crumbs?

_____

What words were used to describe the crumbs?

_____

What would you have done if you had found the cookie crumbs in your bed?

_____

What foods leave crumbs when you eat them in bed?

_____

What creatures eat crumbs for food?

_____

What is the name of the story about children who find their way home by following crumbs?

_____

What foods taste good cooked in bread crumbs?

_____

Poor Pop

Use information from the poem "Song of the Pop-Bottlers" and your own ideas to complete the page.

What does Pop do?

_____

Where does he do this job?

_____

What accident does Pop have?

_____

What happens to the pop-bottles when Pop drops them?

_____

What does Pop do to clean up?

_____

Why do you think Pop has all this trouble?

_____

Where else could Pop work?

_____

74

Pop Words

Circle the words that have the letters "op" in them.
There are 16 words in the word search.

s	h	o	p	d	r	o	p
r	o	p	e	n	p	o	p
o	p	p	o	p	p	y	w
f	l	o	p	t	o	p	s
c	n	s	l	m	o	p	t
l	t	i	e	w	x	r	x
i	x	t	o	p	s	o	v
p	n	e	p	h	o	p	e
s	t	o	p	x	o	n	p
e	t	n	x	o	p	e	n

Choose two words from the puzzle and write sentences using each word.

1. _____

_____

2. _____

_____

What's in Here?

List things that come in these different packages.

Bottles

_____

_____

_____

_____

_____

Boxes

_____

_____

_____

_____

Bags

_____

_____

_____

_____

Jars

_____

_____

_____

_____

Cans

_____

_____

_____

_____

Baskets

_____

_____

_____

_____

I Love the Seasons

Use your own ideas to complete the page.

Places where it's sun and rain and sun again:

_____

_____

Places where there's ice and snow:

_____

_____

Places where the seasons change:

_____

_____

In summer I like to _____

_____

In winter I like to _____

_____

In fall I like to _____

_____

In spring I like to _____

_____

Match the Seasons

Print the words that fit the correct season under each title.

Spring

Summer

Fall

Winter

skiing	toboggan	skating	Thanksgiving
mittens	swim suits	snowmen	coloured leaves
buds	swimming	bonfires	sailing
cottage	camp	Easter	kites
robins	hockey	Halloween	football
flowers	rain	pumpkins	frost

A Poem for the Season

Write a poem about each season.

Fall

_____

_____

_____

_____

Winter

_____

_____

_____

_____

Spring

_____

_____

_____

_____

Summer

_____

_____

_____

_____

Make one of your poems into a shape poem.

Sleighs of Long Ago

Write some of the things you can remember about the sleighs in the story "The Sleighs of Old Montreal."

The Milk Sleigh: _____

_____

_____

_____

The Bread Sleigh: _____

_____

_____

_____

The "Star" Sleigh: _____

_____

_____

_____

The Farmer's Sleigh: _____

_____

_____

_____

The Fire-Hose Sleigh: _____

_____

_____

_____

The Chip Wagon: _____

_____

_____

_____

The Sightseeing Sleigh: _____

_____

_____

_____

If we had sleighs today, I would like to have these two sleighs:

_____

because _____

_____

Words That Grow

Add the letters "er" and "est" to the underlined words to complete the sentences.

Example:

I went on a <u>long</u> sleigh ride.

He went on a _____longer_____ sleigh ride.

She went on the _____longest_____ sleigh ride.

My soup is <u>hot</u>.

His soup is _____

Her soup is the _____

I am a <u>tall</u> person.

My sister is _____ than me.

My brother is the _____ person in our family.

The boy had a <u>big</u> dog.

The girl had a _____ dog.

The man had the _____ dog of all.

The boy heard a <u>loud</u> noise.

The noise became _____

It was the _____ noise he had ever heard.

I can jump <u>high</u>.

My friend can jump _____ than me.

My father can jump the _____ of us all.

Sleigh Questions

Use information from the story "The Sleighs of Old Montreal" and your own ideas to complete the page.

Why did the milk horse move on without the milkman?

_____

_____

Children used to eat frozen milk for fun. What do you eat for fun?

_____

_____

What sleigh did children used to steal rides on?

_____

How do we get our newspapers today?

_____

Here are two things about the farmer who drove his sleigh to market:

_____

_____

What happened when the fire alarm rang?

_____

_____

What could someone buy from the chip wagon?

_____

_____

What did the sightseeing sleigh look like?

_____

_____

My Feet Roll

"My Feet Roll" is a story that is told with pictures.
Choose four pictures from the story and write
what the people in the pictures might be saying.

Picture 1: _____

_____

_____

_____

Picture 2: _____

_____

_____

_____

Picture 3: _____

_____

_____

_____

Picture 4: _____

_____

_____

_____

Moving Along

There are many ways of moving through the world.
Write a word that describes how each thing moves.

Example:

A bird   _flies_

A swimmer   _____

A rabbit   _____

A baby   _____

A jogger   _____

A skier   _____

A motorcycle   _____

A horse   _____

A frog   _____

A snake   _____

Wayne Gretzky   _____

A ballerina   _____

A bull   _____

A mountain climber   _____

An eagle   _____

A duck   _____

A train   _____

Double Letters

Bill and Jill use words with double letters, like the word "kitten."
Circle the words in the list that they would use.

bottles	saddle	goldfish	jello
barrels	bubble	pepper	cake
luggage	ribbon	spaghetti	fish
puppets	pizza	apples	better
hamburger	records	shell	dress
masks	dolls	marry	water
socks	pencils	jelly	puppy
button	zipper	little	sky

Add other words that could be on the list:

_____   _____   _____

_____   _____   _____

_____   _____   _____

A Better World

you were in a wheelchair like the girl in "My Feet Roll,"
what things would make it easier
or you to move around?

How could a curb on a street corner be changed
o help you cross the street?

_____

_____

How would you move through a building with stairs?

_____

_____

How would you get into a bus or car?

_____

What would help you move around at a restaurant?

_____

How would you change your bedroom?

_____

_____

How could your friends help you at school?

_____

_____

Looking for Christmas

Use information from the story "How Six Found Christmas" to complete the page.

Where did the little girl set out to look for Christmas?

_____

_____

What was the one thing the cat wanted to know about Christmas?

_____

_____

What was the one thing the dog wanted to know about Christmas?

_____

_____

What was the one thing the hawk wanted to know about Christmas?

_____

_____

What was the one thing the fox wanted to know about Christmas?

_____

_____

What was the one thing the mockingbird wanted to know about Christmas?

_____

_____

The girl thought the bottle was a Christmas because _____

_____

The cat thought the bottle was a Christmas because _____

_____

The dog thought the bottle was a Christmas because _____

_____

The hawk thought the bottle was a Christmas because _____

_____

The fox thought the bottle was a Christmas because _____

_____

The mockingbird thought the bottle was a Christmas because _____

_____

You know that you have found Christmas when you _____

_____

Thoughtful Christmas Gifts

This list of Christmas gifts has some spelling mistakes.
Print the correct word on the line.

a silver **doller** _____

a new **calendur** _____

a turkey **dinnur** _____

a movie **tickut** _____

a **lovly** doll _____

a blue **ribbin** _____

a Christmas **stoking** _____

a sharp **pencul** _____

a toy **truc** _____

a Christmas **wreeth** _____

a stuffed **animul** _____

a **nuw** book _____

a **grate** big smile _____

a fun **gam** _____

Oh Christmas Tree!

Unscramble the words and print the answers on the lines below.
Start with the underlined letters.

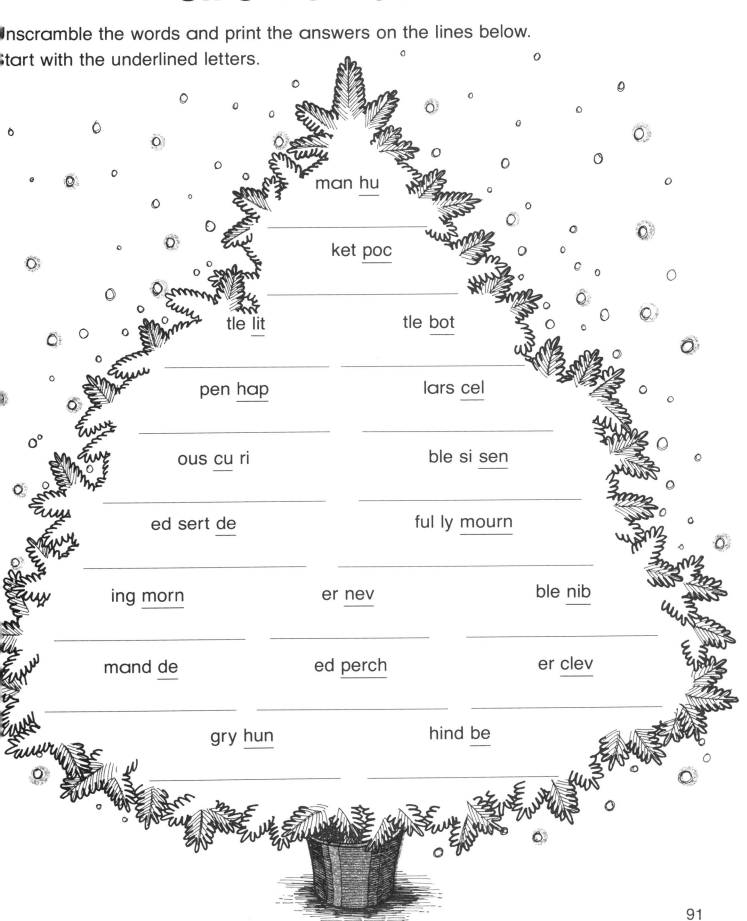

man hu

_____

ket poc

_____

tle lit   tle bot

_____   _____

pen hap   lars cel

_____   _____

ous cu ri   ble si sen

_____   _____

ed sert de   ful ly mourn

_____   _____

ing morn   er nev   ble nib

_____   _____   _____

mand de   ed perch   er clev

_____   _____   _____

gry hun   hind be

_____   _____

Wish a Wish

Can you write a poem about wishing for something?

I will wish for a _____

and a _____

You can wish for a _____

and a _____

But if we both wish

for _____

and _____
We will be friends.

I will blow _____

You can follow _____
Together we will wish

for _____
And be friends
wherever we are.

Do Not Open Until Christmas!

Use information from the story and your own ideas to complete the page.

Why did Gregory have to stay in bed even though he was awake?

_____

_____

_____

_____

What presents had Gregory made for his family?

_____

_____

_____

What present have you made for someone?

_____

_____

What did the sticker say on the big box?

_____

_____

Would you have waited for your parents to wake up
before you opened a Christmas gift?

_____

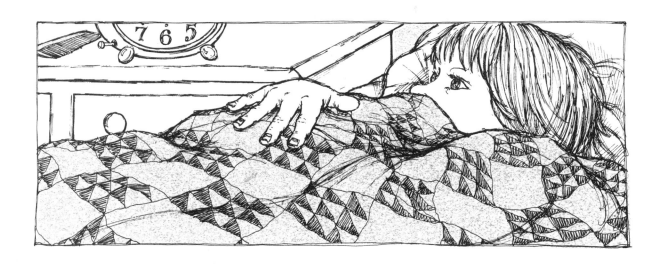

What presents did Gregory get for Christmas?

_____

_____

_____

Why was Gregory's mother angry with him?

_____

_____

_____

Did this story have a happy ending? Why?

_____

_____

If you were Gregory, what would you do next Christmas?

_____

_____

What present would you buy for a dog?

_____

What present would you buy for a child your own age?

_____

Try Again

Can you think of another way to write these sentences?

Example:

Gregory raced in and woke up his parents.

Gregory ran in and woke up his parents.
_____

Gregory curled up under the covers.

_____

He shot out of bed to check the time.

_____

What could he do to make the time pass?

_____

_____

Holly loved dressing up.

_____

Gregory paused at Holly's door.

_____

The package felt like something to wear.

_____

_____

The present had such an interesting rattle.

At once he knew he had done a terrible thing.

Holly saved Christmas for them.

He still could not understand his mother.

Gregory tensed, waiting, watching.

Her face was shining with joy, with love.

She had not shared his delight in the boots.

Friendly Presents

Use information from the poem "If I want I can give it to a friend" and your own ideas to complete the page.

Name three free gifts that were talked about in the poem.

_____

_____

_____

What are some free gifts that you could give to your friends?

_____

_____

_____

What are some gifts that you could make for a friend?

_____

_____

_____

Name some favourite gifts that a friend has given you.

_____

_____

A Song for Twelve Days

Use your own ideas to write a song about the twelve days of Christmas.
Try to think of three things to receive on each day.

On the first day of Christmas
my true love gave to me

_____

_____

_____

On the second day of Christmas
my true love gave to me

_____

_____

_____

On the third day of Christmas
my true love gave to me

_____

_____

_____

On the fourth day of Christmas
my true love gave to me

_____

_____

_____

On the fifth day of Christmas
my true love gave to me

_____

_____

_____

On the sixth day of Christmas
my true love gave to me

_____

_____

_____

On the seventh day of Christmas
my true love gave to me

_____

_____

_____

On the eighth day of Christmas
my true love gave to me

_____

_____

_____

On the ninth day of Christmas
my true love gave to me

_____

_____

_____

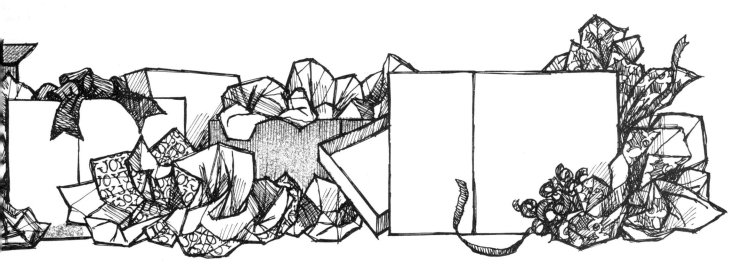

On the tenth day of Christmas
my true love gave to me

_____

_____

_____

_____

On the eleventh day of Christmas
my true love gave to me

_____

_____

_____

On the twelfth day of Christmas
my true love gave to me

_____

_____

_____

As Different as Day and Night

Think about the story "Day and Night: How They Came to Be."
Use your own words to tell each animal's story.

The Fox's Story

You see, I had a magic word _____

_____

_____

_____

_____

The Hare's Story

You see, I had a magic word _____

_____

_____

_____

_____

_____

Adding Words

Make new sentences by writing your own words on the lines.

A word could make something happen.

A _____ word could make something happen.

There was no light on earth yet.

There was no _____ light on earth yet.

Everything was in darkness all the time.

Everything was in _____ darkness all the time.

A fox and a hare had an argument.

A _____ fox and a _____ hare
had an argument.

The hare won.

The _____ hare won.

His word was more powerful.

His _____ word was more powerful.

The word of the fox was powerful too.

The _____ word of the _____ fox
was powerful too.

The nightime of the fox followed the daytime of the hare.

The nightime of the fox followed the daytime of the _____ hare.

Good and Bad

Draw lines to join the opposites.

hot	start	top	bad
stop	deep	good	smooth
shallow	cold	rough	bottom

sit	stand	wide	short
argue	agree	heavy	narrow
walk	run	tall	light

noisy	quiet	neat	full
silly	open	unusual	ordinary
close	clever	empty	messy

Print the opposite of each word.

old _____   light _____

rich _____   sun _____

mean _____   day _____

black _____   fast _____

Magic Words

Can you solve these word puzzles?

Example:

nto - to + side = <u>inside</u>

unlike - like + really - ly = _____

displease - please + cover = _____

read - ad + reader - er = _____

unwell - well + even = _____

discover - cover + like = _____

inside - side + tomorrow - morrow = _____

unless - less + made = _____

inland - land + deed = _____

read - ad + runt - t = _____

undo - do + usual = _____

dislike - like + cover = _____

unripe - ripe + tie = _____

An Arctic Dictionary

You are going to make an Arctic dictionary. Use information from the story "The Arctic: What Lives There" to write a definition for each word.

pack ice: _____

plankton: _____

diatoms: _____

krill: _____

_____

breathing holes: _____

_____

blubber: _____

tundra: _____

_____

snow goose: _____

caribou: _____

musk oxen: _____

lemming: _____

northern lights: _____

_____

Hot and Cold

Print each word in the column it belongs in.
Then add one new word to each column.

frozen	whale	store	cactus
dark	icy	oasis	sand
tundra	walrus	tent	diatom
apartment	krill	seal	camel
car	streets		

Arctic   Desert   City

_____   _____   _____

_____   _____   _____

_____   _____   _____

_____   _____   _____

_____   _____   _____

_____   _____

_____

Flying High

If the sea gull in the poem "Magic Words to Feel Better" could take you into the ai
what would you see as you looked down on earth?
Write a poem about the things you would see.

The Sea Gull and Me

_____

_____

_____

_____

_____

_____

_____

_____

_____

_____

_____

Changing Places

Number the sentences so that they tell the story of the girl who became a reindeer.

(   ) But whenever she saw a reindeer she felt sad.

(   ) There was once a young girl whose name was Leealaura.

(   ) Two children released her leg from a trap.

(   ) "I just want to become a reindeer and live with you."

(   ) Of all things on earth it is worse to be a human being.

(   ) She looked at herself, and she was a reindeer too!

(   ) "Oh, if only I were a snow goose," said Leealaura.

(   ) One day Leealaura's father came home with a boy and a girl.

(   ) All at once she was caught in a trap.

(   ) "I think I would be happy if I were a rabbit," thought Leealaura.

(   ) One day she decided to return to her old home.

(   ) Her father made her toys to play with and told her stories.

(   ) The reindeer turned into Leealaura the girl.

(   ) The reindeer decided she could become one of them.

Changing Words

In the story "The Girl Who Became a Reindeer," a girl changes into an animal.
Can you change the underlined words into other words?

What letter can you add to <u>one</u> to make another word? _____

Can you find another name in <u>Leealaura</u>? _____

Add two letters to <u>cloth</u> to fill your closet with _____

Change one letter in <u>store</u> and change the weather. _____

What kind of house does the mixed-up word <u>ologi</u> become? _____

Can you find another word in <u>running</u>? _____

Change two letters in <u>goose</u> to make a flock. _____

Change one letter in <u>house</u> to make an animal. _____

If you add a letter to <u>hut</u>, you can search for food to kill. _____

If you can think of a word that sounds the same as <u>pear</u>,

you will have two. _____

Add three letters to <u>appear</u> and make it invisible. _____

Change one letter in <u>roof</u> and give a reindeer a _____

If you change one letter in <u>trip</u> you will be caught in a _____

Leealaura

Use information from the story "The Girl Who Became a Reindeer" to complete the page.

Why did Leealaura leave her home?

_____

_____

Why did Leealaura decide not to become a snow goose?

_____

_____

How did the rabbit convince Leealaura that she would not be happy as a rabbit?

_____

_____

What happened to Leealaura after she stayed with the reindeer overnight?

_____

_____

What happened to Leealaura when she returned to her father's igloo?

_____

_____

Did the story end happily? Why?

_____

_____

Dear Deer

Print the correct word in each line to complete the sentences.

It started to _____ (rain rein)

I visited my _____ (ant aunt)

He hunted the _____ (dear deer)

The ribbon was _____ (red read)

He _____ the answer. (knows nose)

We _____ the turkey. (ate eight)

Dad used lots of _____ to make the cake. (flower flour)

My dress was on _____ (sale sail)

The turtle won the race with the _____ (hare hair)

_____ you help me? (Would Wood)

I'd like a _____ of pie. (piece peace)

It's _____ heavy for me. (to two too)

A _____ is a little insect. (be bee)

I have a _____ of cats. (pear pair)

That is _____ house by the park. (they're their)

A _____ grows in a garden. (flour flower)

Pitseolak's Puzzle

Use words from the story "Pitseolak: Pictures Out of My Life"
to complete the sentences. Then find your answer words in the word search.

1. Pitseolak is an Inuit or ___ ___ ___ ___ ___ ___ word
   for sea pigeon.
2. Pitseolak never saw the monsters and ___ ___ ___ ___ ___ ___
3. Pitseolak drew in the old ___ ___ ___ ___
4. Pitseolak did more than

   a thousand ___ ___ ___ ___ ___ ___ ___
5. Pitseolak had different houses

   for the different ___ ___ ___ ___ ___ ___
6. A house made of ice is called an ___ ___ ___ ___ ___ ___
7. A tent-hut is called a ___ ___ ___ ___ ___
8. Balls were made from ___ ___ ___ ___ ___ ___ ___ skins.
9. In the old days Pitseolak was never done

   with the ___ ___ ___ ___ ___ ___

10. Pitseolak used animal ___ ___ ___ ___ ___ to make different things.

c	k	E	s	k	i	m	o	x	s	s
a	s	l	s	o	m	n	o	b	e	p
r	m	m	f	e	b	y	x	t	a	i
i	g	l	o	o	w	a	y	s	s	r
b	t	e	x	p	o	i	n	v	o	i
o	s	k	i	n	s	a	n	e	n	t
u	b	d	r	a	w	i	n	g	s	s
k	a	a	m	u	k	p	n	x	e	e

A Famous Painter

Use information from the story "Pitseolak: Pictures Out of My Life" and your own ideas to complete the page.

Pitseolak's name means _____

What would you like your name to mean?

_____

_____

Pitseolak likes to draw _____

_____

_____

What do you like to draw?

_____

_____

_____

Piseolak used to move _____

Have you ever moved to a new place?

_____

_____

Pitseolak used to live in _____

_____

What does your house look like?

_____

_____

Pitseolak used to play Eskimo tennis by _____

_____

_____

Tell about a game you like to play.

_____

_____

_____

Pitseolak used to sew _____

_____

Have you ever sewn anything?

_____

_____

How would you tell someone what Pitseolak's pictures look like?

_____

_____

_____

Frozen Words

These words got so cold that some of the letters froze and disappeared.
Can you find them and make complete words again?

___ rt ___ st: a person, like Pitseolak, who draws pictures

l ___ v ___ l ___: this means beautiful or delightful

th ___ ___ s ___ nd: one more than 999

s ___ gn ___ d: to write your name on a letter or painting

w ___ ___ th ___ ___: snow, rain, sunny, windy

s ___ ___ s ___ ns: fall, winter, spring, summer

___ gl ___ ___: a house in the Arctic

s ___ ___: a body of water

c ___ r ___ b ___ ___: an animal that lives in the Arctic

w ___ lr ___ s: an animal with big tusks

k ___ y ___ k: a kind of canoe

p ___ ct ___ r ___ s: the things Pitseolak drew

sp ___ r ___ ts: another word for ghosts

p ___ g ___ ___ n: a bird

Husky Dogs

In the story "A Gift for Kuni," you find out many things about husky dogs.
Make a booklet about husky dogs for other people to read.
What do they eat? Where do they live? What do they look like?

1. _____

_____

2. _____

_____

3. _____

_____

4. _____

_____

_____

5. _____

_____

_____

6. _____

_____

_____

7. _____

_____

_____

8. _____

_____

_____

9. _____

_____

_____

10. _____

_____

Winter Dreams

Can you explain the expressions that are underlined in the sentences?

His mind was <u>buzzing with excitement</u>.

_____

_____

Cheno's <u>ice-blue eyes</u> looked at everyone.

_____

_____

Cheno is <u>a natural born leader</u>.

_____

_____

You must eat or <u>your strength will fade</u>.

_____

_____

The boy worried <u>as the day slipped by</u>.

_____

_____

The winds made their way into Kuni's dreams.

_____

Cheno was feeling like part of the family.

_____

_____

Kuni buried his face in the dog's long fur.

_____

The boy was so happy he could hardly speak.

_____

_____

He settled down for the rest of the night.

_____

_____

Broken Words

Join the pieces of cracked ice with a line to make a word.
Then print the words.

		mukluks
muk	vens	
pack	luks	_____
ra	ing	_____
win	ter	_____
trap	turn	_____
re	sled	_____
dog	ping	_____
sum	mer	_____
scat	tens	_____
mit	ter	_____
fall	gled	_____
sup	en	_____
strug	plied	_____
rab	mon	_____
com	bits	_____

A Winter Story

Use information from the story "Children of the Yukon" and your own ideas to complete the page.

As regular as winter, the _____ return to the towns.

In my town, the _____ return every winter.

In Dawson City, the children make _____ in winter.

In my town, we make _____

_____

On Nares Lake, the children play around a _____

_____

In my town, we play around _____

_____

In the Yukon, the sound of children laughing means _____

_____

In my town, the sound of _____

_____

In February on the frozen Yukon River, the children watch ————

————

In my town, we all watch ————

————

On Crag Lake, boys help their fathers ————

————

In my town, children help their parents ————

————

In the Yukon, they use rabbit fur for ————

————

In my town, our mittens and boots are ————

————

In the Yukon, a common greeting is, ————

————

In my town, a common greeting is, ————

————

In the Yukon

Match the sentences with the correct word or words.

Example:

1. They return to the towns.   (I) ravens

2. They throw food to the ravens.   (   ) Crag Lake

3. It comes early to the Yukon.   (   ) children

4. Darkness falls on it.   (   ) Yukon River

5. They make snowmen.   (   ) mushers

6. It is too powdery for packing.   (   ) boats

7. Children haul water from them.   (   ) snow

8. It is a retired paddlewheeler.   (   ) ice holes

9. They were used before roads were built. (   ) moose

10. It makes people laugh and trip.   (   ) S.S. Tutshi

11. They race huskies.   (   ) children

12. Races are held on it.   (   ) winter

13. Fish are caught in it.   (   ) snowshoe rabbit

14. It is snared for food and fur.   (   ) snowshoes

15. It provides meat.   (   ) Dawson City

Whale Words

Print your favourite words from each of the poems in "There's a Sound in the Sea."

Here come the whales:

_____

_____

Silly and funny:

_____

_____

Swish, swish:

_____

_____

The men kill the whale:

_____

_____

The moonlight fell upon her head:

_____

_____

Write a poem about a whale.

Use your own words and some of your favourite ones from the poems.

Draw a picture to go with your poem.

Quiz Time

Can you answer these questions about some of the stories and poems in the reader?

What did Simon try to catch?

_____

Who liked to solve crimes?

_____

Whose house was the party at?

_____

What poem was about soup?

_____

What was Pop's job?

_____

What city had sleighs?

_____

How many tried to find Christmas?

_____

What was Kuni's gift?

_____

What famous artist lived in the North?

_____

Thinking About Myself

This year the best story I read was _____

_____

because _____

_____

This year the best story I listened to was _____

_____

because _____

_____

This year the best movie I saw was _____

_____

because _____

_____

This year the best picture I painted was _____

_____

because _____

_____